Project Boaz:

Leave a Little Extra Behind…

What is Boaz's Motivation?

Dr. Darryl Claybon

To: Aletheia

From: Dr. D.C.

6/24/22

Project Boaz

Leave a Little Extra Behind...What is Boaz's Motivation?

Trilogy Christian Publishers

A Wholly Owned Subsidiary of Trinity Broadcasting Network

2442 Michelle Drive

Tustin, CA 92780

For information, address Trilogy Christian Publishing

Rights Department, 2442 Michelle Drive, Tustin, CA 92780.

Trilogy Christian Publishing/ TBN and colophon are trademarks of Trinity Broadcasting Network.

For information about special discounts for bulk purchases, please contact Trilogy Christian Publishing.

Manufactured in the United States of America

10 9 8 7 6 5 4 3 2 1

Library of Congress Cataloging-in-Publication Data is available.

ISBN: 978-1-68556-763-7

ISBN: 978-1-68556-764-4

DEDICATION

To God be the Glory, the Honor, and the Praise.

*"Just let me live my life And let it be pleasing,
Lord to Thee And should I gain any praise,
Let it go to Calvary."*

Andrae Crouch

PREFACE

The purpose of this book is to explore the steps taken and the steps that can be taken, to make a difference in the lives of those that would benefit the most.

The work is divided into three sections. Section 1: **The Biblical Perspective** provides the basis upon which the idea of "leaving a little extra behind" is derived. In this biblical account, Boaz directs his workers to leave extra grain in the field on purpose. We explore his motivation. The second section deals with **The Practical Perspective"** of carrying out this premise. It is just one way some persons in the twenty-first century are living out this first-century notion. The third section is **The Visionary Perspective.** We are called to be mindful and courageous when assisting others. However, that is not the end of the story. We must envision and embrace a better day for everyone.

The proposed vision may seem ludicrous in this day and time. Perhaps as outrageous as crossing a red sea or feeding over five thousand persons with two fish and five barley loaves. But the cost of "no vision" has far-reaching consequences. Perhaps it is true: no person is an island, and where there is no vision, the people perish.

ACKNOWLEDGMENTS

To my Wonderful Parents James & Dorothy Claybon, To my Professors, Coaches, Mentors, Colleagues and Pastors. To Bishop Thomas & Dr. Louise Baker-Brown, Presiding Elder Lindsey & Mrs. Phyllis Waitts Napier, College of Bishops, and our Friends at Trilogy Christian Publishing (TBN) for the opportunity of a lifetime. To my Family, Friends, eCentering-Moments Family, Pastor Daniel Perry for the Logo Design, & to the members of this congregation, thank all of you for teaching me about faith and courage under fire. I never would have made it without you. To my students: Thank you for the moments when "the student became the teacher," and "this teacher became your student." I am eternally grateful! Darryl "Dr. C" Claybon

The question to Pontius Pilate is: "Why did you write that inscription?" Pilate's reply, was as mine is, "ἀπεκρίθη ὁ Πιλᾶτος ὃ γέγραφα γέγραφα" Pilate answered, "What I have written I have written." John 19:22 (KJV)

INTRODUCTION:

"Leave a little extra behind" is a philosophy, a principle, and a proverb found in every culture around the globe. Every city, state, and nation worldwide engage in comforting and sharing with those dealing with life's unexplained and devastating circumstances. In every hamlet, town, and village, we find a part of society encountering some unfortunate situations thru no fault of their own.

On every street, every road, every lane, every path, paved or unpaved, rocky or smooth, wide or narrow, one lane or two, roads with a bridge and without a bridge, there is at least one person who finds oneself in need. If one has not found a time when they are in need, as explained to this author, "just keep on living!"

TABLE OF CONTENTS:

PROLOGUE

The purpose of this section is an attempt to explain Boaz's motivation for providing food, shelter, protection, and a future for Ruth. Is it love, compassion, or something more than our human hearts can comprehend?

The writer of the book of Ruth never mentions the word "love." So, as Tina Turner asks, "What's love got to do with it (3)?" Or perhaps Pat Benatar is right, for she declares, "Love is a Battlefield (4)!"

SECTION ONE:

BIBLICAL PERSPECTIVE

In these heartbreaking moments, we find Naomi experiencing what appears to be a series of serious setbacks and situations.

SETTING

In our story, Naomi and her family are moving to Moab, which is about fifty miles east of the city of Bethlehem. The reason they are moving is that there is a famine in the town of Bethlehem. Ironically, Bethlehem means "House of Bread," and the House of Bread has run out of bread. So, she, her husband, and two sons load up the wagon and move to Moab. While there, her sons find wives, and they all settle in a suburb often referred to as "happily ever after."

SITUATION

However, something strange happens in the story. The writer tells us that first, Naomi's husband passes away. We are not given any indication of what happened. We are not sure if it is a sudden or a gradual illness. Then, to make matters worse, after ten years of living in Moab, both of Naomi's sons pass away. Again, the writer does not indicate the cause of it being gradual, sudden, or hereditary.

It is at this point; Naomi decides to return to Bethlehem. As she leaves for Bethlehem, one of her daughters-in-law, Orpah, chooses to stay in Moab. Perhaps this daughter-in-law thinks her chances would be better in her hometown, and therefore she stays behind.

Naomi speaks to her other daughter-in-law Ruth saying, I would understand if you decided to stay. Ruth replies, "No, I'm going to stay with you. Wherever you go, I shall go, and whatever God you serve, I will serve. Wherever you die, I will die."

Naomi and Ruth return to Bethlehem. The town is buzzing with the news. Some are asking, "Is that Naomi, after all this time?" Naomi's response is alarming but somewhat understandable. She changes her name, saying, "Don't call me Naomi which means, beauty, but call me Mara, which means bitter." For she says, the Lord has dealt her a bitter blow. "I left here full, but now I am back with only the clothes on my back" (NIV). It is obviously clear who Naomi is bitter with because of her losses. First, there is the loss of her husband, two sons, and one daughter-in-law. Her worries are compounded by food insecurities, financial instabilities, and a future filled with uncertainties. Indeed, a bitter blow!

Ruth, on the other hand, decides to go to work. As a foreigner in Bethlehem, she can only find a job in a field gleaning after the harvesters. After going from field to field, she finally finds work in an area owned by Boaz. Her decision helps us understand that sometimes we must take what we are presented with until we can get what we want.

She works all morning without taking a break. Around this time, Boaz, the owner of the field, arrives. He sees Ruth and begins to inquire about her. Boaz asks his workers, "Who is she, and how did she get here?" The workers reply that she is "Naomi's daughter-in-law" and notably add that she has been working all day without even taking a break.

*Boaz approaches Ruth saying, "My daughter,
listen to me. Don't go and glean in another field
and don't go away from here. Stay here with
the women who work for me (Ruth 2: 9, NIV)*

Boaz tells Ruth to stay in his field, work with the
other women in his area, and not leave his domain. He
also tells her to drink water from the barrels that the
other workers gather at break time—an incredible act of
kindness.

Notice at this time, Ruth's curiosity awakens; she
bows to the ground and asks, "What have I done to
deserve such favor? How is it that you have noticed me a
foreigner?" (Ruth 2: 10, NIV)

Boaz replies, "I've been told all about what you have
done for your mother-in-law since the death of your
husband—how you left your father and mother and your
homeland and came to live with a people you did not
know before."

Then Boaz begins to speak a blessing over her
life. He says, "May the Lord repay you for your acts
of kindness." Further, he offers, "May you be richly,
deeply, and suitably rewarded and repaid, by the Lord,
the God of Israel, under whose wings you have come to
take refuge (Ruth 2: 11-12, NIV)."

Ruth responds by saying, "May I continue to find
favor in your eyes, my Lord. You have made me feel
comfortable by being kind to your servant, though I am
not one of your servants. You have touched my heart and
treated me as one of your own, and I don't even belong

here!" Ruth is aware at all times of the challenges that she faces. It is apparent she takes nothing for granted. She recognizes when she is being blessed.

At lunchtime, Boaz goes a step further. He brings lunch to Ruth so she can eat. She eats until she is full, and the writer shares with us, there is bread leftover. An indication that the famine in Bethlehem is over. The season of lack will turn to the season of abundance.

When Ruth gets up to go back to work, Boaz directs his workers to leave a little extra behind.

> *16 When she got up to go back to work, Boaz ordered his servants: "Let her glean where there's still plenty of grain on the ground— make it easy for her. Better yet, pull some of the good stuff out and leave it for her to glean. Give her special treatment (Ruth 2:16, NIV)."*

Centering Moment 1- Time and space for reflection.

Please take time to

Center Yourself

by answering the following Centering Questions:

CENTERING QUESTIONS

1. So, what is Boaz's motivation? Why is he so interested in Ruth?

2. Is this love or genuine concern? Is concern the same as love?

3. What about the other workers? Did Boaz show them special treatment, or is it only Ruth? If so, is this fair?

4. Are Naomi and Ruth's problems caused by personal decisions, or is this what we call "unfortunate circumstances?"

Your Thoughts and Answers

Theological Crimes or High Misdemeanors: Elements of the story that cannot be explained but are essential to the outcome of the story. (Claybon, 2021)
Are there elements or parts of this story that cannot be explained?

SOLUTIONS

Perhaps we can never know Boaz's motivation.
As we understand it, his motives may include matters of
the heart, mind, and soul. Those instincts and initiatives,
perhaps too, are beyond human apprehension and
comprehension.

The Apostle Paul refers to "have apprehended it not"
that which has "apprehended him (NIV)." Perhaps Paul
is saying something holds him spiritually, mentally,
and physically captive, and that captivity for himself is
inescapable:

Phillips 3:12-13

> [12] *Not as though I had already attained, either
> were already perfect: but I follow after, if
> that may apprehend that for which also I am
> apprehended of Christ Jesus.* [13] *Brethren, I
> count not myself to have apprehended: but
> this one thing I do, forgetting those things
> which are behind, and reaching forth unto
> those things which are before. (KJV)*

But thank God this is not how the story ends.
There is some good news in the text. Leaders can find
some valuable lessons by examining the relationships
between Naomi, Ruth, and Boaz.

Notice the

Investigation

Invitation

Improvisation

A-Investigation

Leaders are concerned about their Teams and Communities

Leaders are informed, interested, and invested in their Teams and their Communities. Boaz sees Ruth and immediately begins to study, research, and probe into her background. Asking "What is her story? What information is available about her?"

Often there are many assumptions made about others. A conclusion is drawn almost immediately based on a person's perceived appearance. Boaz seeks the facts about Ruth's situation. Boaz can now make an informed decision, and not on emotions alone.

B-Invitation

Leaders Connect with the members of their Team and Communities

He invites her to the table and provides necessary life-sustaining essentials. Notice how Boaz provides for her physical and social needs first. He realizes Ruth must be thirsty, hungry, and feeling alone. Here, Boaz is perhaps operating on more than an assumption or an opinion. Boaz can determine by his investigation and no doubt confirmed by his discernment, intellect, and essential human compassion, this is the case.

So often, persons in need must ask for help. It would stand to reason, if a person has ever been in a similar situation, recognizing someone in need should not be difficult.

Many times, help is not received because of the way it is offered. Offering help without providing dignity and respect is "like pouring water on a drowning person." If one is giving support without heart-driven, or heart-filled empathy, it is, as the writer of 2 Corinthians says, just sounding brass and tinkling cymbals.

In Pastoral Care Courses, Evangelism Classes, and Missionary Preparation Webinars, we teach students to "never blame the victim for being the victim. "Trouble comes to all!"

It is easy to ask, "How did I get yourself into this situation?"

What were you thinking? Didn't you know better?

How long are you going to live like this?

A better question: How can I assist you at this time?

C Improvisation- Leaders show Compassion Now

Instructs workers to leave a little extra behind.

We are all blown away beyond measure as Boaz responds. Please note there is an immediate solution to this series of serious, sad, and debilitating situations. Boaz operates under the umbrella of "right now management." He Manages the Moment.

"Managing the Moment" dwells only on the past for the present's sake. The past provides guiding principles but does not prolong progress. It answers the question, what can I do right now! The key to Managing the Moment is improvisation. It is crucial because it considers all the known factors, devises a plan, and implements it immediately.

Without hesitation, Boaz is moved to provide for Ruth's immediate need of food, water, and companionship. Then takes measures to secure her need for job stability and personal security.

He instructs his workers to protect Ruth and ensure that a little extra grain is left in the field for her to glean. He provides it in such a way that she can receive this blessing with dignity and respect.

> *What then shall we say to these things...?*
> *(Romans 8:31*, KJV)

In the next following pages, you will find a ministry inspired by the story of Naomi, Ruth, and Boaz.

Sources

King James Version (KJV)

Holy Bible, New International Version®, NIV® Copyright ©1973, 1978, 1984, 2011 by Biblica, Inc.® Used by permission. All rights reserved worldwide.

SECTION TWO:

A PRACTICAL
PERSPECTIVE

PROJECT BOAZ: LEAVE A LITTLE EXTRA BEHIND

A NEW ERA OF EVANGELISTS AND MISSIONARIES

In our town, located over 130 miles southwest of a great metropolis, lies a great community severely impacted by the Covid-19 pandemic. The community was already struggling with dire economic challenges and crucial, devastating social issues, as were all communities.

However, the COVID-19 pandemic deals a "bitter blow" to the marketplace of the town's citizens and economy. The small-town has seen hard times, but these current times are more complex, more demanding, and more challenging. Many families face insurmountable economic losses, job instability, food insecurity, inescapable health concerns, a declining population, closed sanctuaries, technology constraints, and very little hope.

The choices the remnant of this mighty congregation faced were few. Do we save the children, save the community, or save the church which has been closed for the past eighteen months? The children need a reminder that someone cares. Local business owners need a lifeline to remain open. The church building needs repairing and assistance to implement CDC standards. Further complicating these dire situations, the church coffers have "less than two fish and no barley loaves."

But there is good news…

The congregation could have walked away from their church and community. However, the handful of remaining members, subscribe to an everlasting faith that the German Theologian **Friedrich Schleiermacher** describes it as "Absolute Dependence on God (1)." The Congregation explains it as their Sacred Theology known as "A Way Out of No Way!"

The devoted members have a different mindset and a different question.

Their question was not, "What can the community do for us?" Instead, their question was, "What can we do for our community?"

Thus, is born a New Era of Evangelist and Missionaries. The members find a new way of caring and connecting with their neighbors and local business owners. Church members began to personally build a bridge to the entire community served by the Church.

If D.T. Niles is right: "Evangelism is one beggar telling another where to find bread (1)." Then it would stand to reason that Community Evangelism can be described as one beggar, bringing bread to another beggar, the bread they have found. (Claybon, 2021)

HOW IT STARTED

While working with various Back-to-School programs, the congregation appreciated the efforts of everyone in the community providing backpacks, clothes, shoes, and school supplies for students and teachers. However, for students, haircuts and hairstyles are often overlooked.

The small, but faithful congregation believed that proper grooming wasn't just about looking presentable; it also affected one's self-esteem.

"We wanted children to have a quality haircut and hairstyling so they can feel good about themselves, inside and out." With that newfound self-confidence, they can excel in their studies and live happier lives!

So, we partnered with the barber shop and hair salon in our community.

HOW IT WORKS:

1. While visiting your local Barbershop or Hair Salon,
Leave behind the price of

   1 Child's Haircut or Hairstyle.
   Just "1"

   The barber or stylist will know which child will benefit the most from a free haircut or hairstyle.

2. As the child/child's parents are paying for the services rendered:

   The barber or stylist will say "The haircut/ hairstyle today, is a gift from (Insert your Church name) and this shop/salon" and present the business card.

   (You can print business cards/or small card with Church info or your personal business)

Alternatively, there are two other options

Your congregation can partner with a local barber shop or hair stylist in your congregation or community.

1. Pay in advance and let the barbers/stylists choose the child/children that will benefit the most

   Or

2. Church provide tickets to parent/ child/children that benefit the most:

   (Via schools, social workers, etc.)

a. Children present tickets to Stylist/barber

b. A member/Minister goes Weekly to shop/ pick up and pay for tickets.

c. Or barber/stylist can text ticket number and payment sent thru Cash App.

Accounting

At this point your barber/stylist will text or call you saying, "One haircut, done!" or "One hairstyle, done."

Then, if you are a member of a group or team, please text your Team Captain.

As a result, your gift will:

1. Strengthen the confidence of the children.

2. Strengthen the confidence of the barbers and stylists' Business,

3. Strengthen the confidence of your community in your Church.

   O The Church will initiate the gift of giving and empower both children, families, and businesses in your local community.

   O A bond is formed between the Church, the local barbers, and stylists.

   O The barbers and stylists become the New Era of Evangelists and missionaries for your congregation.

A Blessing for Children and Parents:

The Children and Parents will never forget.

They will always remember this act of kindness.
In this time of job instability, and food insecurity, and
spiritual ambiguity, an act of service such as this is
welcome. **For parents,** it is a sign of hope to the least,
less, and left out: the God in the Church Building is
the God in the Community. They will remember this
blessing coming at a time the parents really need it.

ECENTERING-MOMENT I

*[15] And when the children of Israel saw it, they
said one to another, It is manna: for they
knew not what it was. And Moses said unto
them, this is the bread which the LORD hath
given you to eat. (Exodus 16:15, NIV)*

After the Israelites were freed from bondage and
wandering in the wilderness. Some would say the
Israelites were trying to find their future. They received a
blessing of bread. It was something strange, with an odd
shape. They called it Manna, for they did not know it
was Bread. Moses told them "It is Bread from heaven."

O Can blessing come in different shapes and sizes?

O Did the Israelites ever forget this Blessing?

The Children's Laughter

The children, with newfound confidence, will begin to take on the task of forging their own identities. Too often this process is left to the proponents of social media in their quest to define cultures. There were times when societal lessons taught in the home superseded peer pressure.

However, now it seems that those same lessons are overridden, ignored, and canceled by today's trending social media's "video gone viral." It is easy to get the message that says showing kindness and empathy is the same as showing weakness.

Also, inspiring confidence in a hectic world will ultimately lead to a bright future. A person who realizes their self-worth increases their chances of self-fulfilled development to thrive. They will become trailblazers, business owners, professional athletes, principals, teachers, real estate developers, and world changers!

There is a chance with our help, they will gain an understanding of the principles of grooming. Armed with this knowledge and well-being, they will become productive citizens. They may eventually make their way to the door of the Church that helped "make a way out of no way!"

CENTERING-MOMENTS II:

[21] *"And I will make the Egyptians favorably disposed toward this people, so that when you leave you will not go empty-handed. [22] Every woman is to ask her neighbor and any woman living in her house for articles of silver and gold and for clothing, which you will put on your sons and daughters. (Exodus 3:21-22, NIV)*

In the verses above, God is giving Moses some instructions. After four hundred and twenty years, God delivers the Israelites from Egypt and the hand of Pharoah. The Israelites will not walk away empty-handed but be blessed with silver, gold, and clothing.

Why do you think the Israelites are asked to dress up the Children?

O So, the children can have a new mindset.

O So, the children can see themselves in a positive light.

O Grooming boosts the confidence of children.

O All the above?

A Blessing for the Barbers and Stylist

The barber and stylist will never forget. They, too, have suffered tremendous losses. The aftermath of the Covid-19 pandemic has resulted in an array of negative emotions whereas these issues, have been difficult to overcome. Some shops and salons, like some Churches, will never reopen. But this is not how their story has to end.

Barbers and stylists are still the gatekeepers in the community. The church can partner with these persons who have their fingers on the pulse of the community. They can identify and pass the blessing on to the parents and children in a non-embarrassing holistic way.

Some people in need do not come forward and receive a blessing or gift because of the way it is presented. Most stylists and barbers know how to make people feel comfortable. We can trust their professionalism to carry out this mission with the necessary discretion.

CENTERING-MOMENT III

> *Each of you are to take up a stone on your shoulder, according to the number of the tribes of the Israelites, ⁶ to serve as a sign among you. In the future, when your children ask you, 'What do these stones mean?' (Joshua 4:4-6)*

In the above verses, the Israelites are asked to remember their deliverance. They created monuments made of stones, so when the children asked, "What is meant by the stones?" The parents can tell the story of their deliverance.

Will the barbers, stylists, children and parents, remember the day the Church "gave unto them" in their time of need?

O Not likely

O Most Likely

A Blessing for the Congregation
Reconnect, Rebuild, and Repair

The Congregation can be the catalyst to reconnect families and rebuild the pipeline of persons joining the Church. Individuals can repair the bridge that leads to a healthier, stronger nation, one village, one community, and one hamlet at a time.

Project Boaz is just one way of rejuvenating, reviving, and restoring both the Church and the community in which it serves. The members of the household of faith can do something once a week, once a month, or even once a year that will change lives forever.

Catalyst for Socioeconomic Recovery

This project proves the Church can be the catalyst to economic and social growth in communities in need of a solution.

Far too long, we have asked shop and salon owners to carry the burden of inspiring our young people with the gift of self-worth and value. We have asked the shop owners to support the Church by "purchasing ads" for our programs.

The shop and salon owners have always responded without hesitation! We now have a chance to make a difference by sowing seeds of grace and mercy into their business.

As the new Era of Evangelists and Missionaries emerge, we can:

- ✓ Bless the children and their parents.
- ✓ Bless the Shop and Salon owners.
- ✓ Bless Congregations with an opportunity to impact and change the lives of the people living in the communities we serve.

And most of all,

God gets all the

Praise, Honor, and the Glory!

Selah

Sources

1. *Scharlemann, R. P. (2021, November 17). Friedrich Schleiermacher. Encyclopedia Britannica. https://www.britannica.com/biography/Friedrich-Schleiermacher*

2. *NIV Holy Bible, New International Version®, NIV® Copyright ©1973, 1978, 1984, 2011 by Biblica, Inc.® Used by permission. All rights reserved worldwide*

3. *Turner, Tina. What's Love got to do with it. Capitol Records 1994.*

4. *Benatar, Pat. Love is a Battlefield. MCA Whitney 1983*

SECTION THREE:

VISIONARY PERSPECTIVE

Plato's Republic, Moore's Utopia
and
Jefferson's Declaration:

A VISION FOR OUR TOWN

Plato's Republic (1), Thomas Moore's Utopia (2), Thomas Jefferson's Declaration of Independence, and the residents of our town, all have one similar goal: They all seek a more perfect Union. A place where there is an opportunity to seek life, liberty, and the pursuit of happiness.

The citizens of our city in 2022, like those of Athens in 375 BCE, Utopia in 1516 CE, and Philadelphia in 1776 CE, are not looking for handouts. But instead, a chance to provide a future for their families. The dedicated people in this wonderful town, hope the opportunities to do so are offered, extended, and accessible with dignity, value, and self-worth.

WHERE TO BEGIN

One of the leading industries in this part of the nation is Solar Farming. According to Renewable Energy World:

"Solar farms are large-scale solar installations where photovoltaic (PV) panels, referred to as solar panels, or other means of collecting solar energy, are used to harvest the sun's power." (Solar Farm 2019)

The project for our town begins by building a solar

farm on the campus of the middle school. By building on the campus the children and teachers can participate in the planning, building, and maintaining of this solar farm. The students and teachers can get "hands-on experience with renewable energy."

Also, at some point, they will switch the power source of the school to solar energy. Any power not used can be sold to the local power company, and the proceeds used to enhance the county school system amenities. Principals, vice-principals, administrators, teachers, and other school employees can also participate and receive additional income upon specialization certifications.

The plan includes showing the young minds and instructors the actual cost of the entire operation. Then, as the students reach High School level and show an interest in new energy sources, they can access further training. There will be classes on land, purchasing, capital, equipment, personnel, training, requisitions, just-in-time inventories, methods for increasing profits and decreasing losses. The list is endless in terms of opportunities.

WHERE IT LEADS

Building Bridges to Institutions of Higher Learning

Further, colleges and universities will be allowed to provide grants and set up data collecting labs. The information collected can be shared with nations all over the world that are shifting to renewable resources.

These institutions of higher learning can assist with scholarships for promising candidates. Also, this provides a pipeline of qualified college students from this county to every college and university in the country.

Those graduates will most likely return home to this city, with experience and expertise if all goes as planned. Notably, the new jobs are providing adequate income in the place they call home.

Finally, there is a way to secure this vision for us and many other small-town USA cities.

Along with the help of the county school system, colleges, and universities, corporations can come in and build a prototype solar-powered restaurant, hotel, retail store, etc

Again, the colleges and universities have built data collection centers.

Therefore, they can also monitor the specific brand performance of each restaurant, hotel, gas station, barbershop, hair salon, etc., and provide real-time cost analysis.

Additionally, Companies may provide renewable energy for their operations and sell unused solar power for a profit. Streamlining cost and increasing profitability is the goal and the gold standard for all successful businesses.

Churches powered by renewable energy can lower their operational costs and assist even more with community needs.

Such a business plan will allow the good people of our township to live in a place where there is an opportunity to seek life, liberty, and the pursuit of happiness.

CALL TO ACTION

(Please insert your name in place of Paul's)

That night Paul had a dream: A Macedonian stood on the far shore and called across the sea, "Come over to Macedonia and help us!" The dream gave Paul his map. We went to work at once, getting things ready to cross over to Macedonia. All the pieces had come together. (Acts 16:9, MSG)

Sources

1. *Plato, Bloom, A. (1968). The Republic. New York: Basic Books.*

2. *More, T., & In Turner, P. (1972). Utopia. Baltimore: Penguin Books.*

3. *What is a Solar Farm? (2019, April 19). Renewable Energy World. Retrieved November 29, 2021, from https://www.renewableenergyworld.com/storage/what-is-a-solar-farm/#gref*

4. *The Message (MSG) Copyright © 1993, 2002, 2018 by Eugene H. Peterson*

Dr. Claybon is Pastor, Coach, ACPE Clinician, Distinguished Professor of Humanities, and author of several books. Along with his three decades of Practical Parish Ministry, he has successfully guided numerous pastors, congregations, and thousands of students in discovering their passion and reclaiming their mission and ministry. For more information, consultation, and webinars, please visit website: projectboaz.com or contact Dr. Claybon at drcitc@gmail.com.

CPSIA information can be obtained
at www.ICGtesting.com
Printed in the USA
BVHW050416310522
638422BV00006B/176